SCRUM

A Step-by-Step Guide to Managing Product
Development

BILL GALVIN

Contents

Introduction

Thank you for purchasing *"SCRUM: A Step-by-Step Guide to Managing Product Development"*. If you are reading this, then you are serious about improving your knowledge of Agile project management methodologies, in particular, Scrum. Also, you are truly serious about how you can improve your overall project management skills.

I am well aware that there are other books out there on this topic. So, your preference is greatly appreciated. I am sure that you will find lots of actionable information in this book. You will not only come again with a good understanding of what Agile and Scrum are but also, you will be able to make a significant shift in mindset so that you may embrace the Agile mindset.

To most folks, Scrum is associated with software development. And while it is true that Agile is a project management framework and Scrum is a project management methodology born out of the software development industry, the fact of the matter is that Scrum has a cross-cutting appeal across various industries and fields of endeavor.

When you embrace the Agile mindset, you will be able to have new and innovative ways of doing business. As such, Agile allows you to make a fundamental shift in mindset such as to accept change as a normal part of life. Instead of being concerned about change and how to reduce the likelihood of it, you will be focused on making the most of the opportunities you have to adopt change and innovate.

Traditional project management methodologies use a system focused on processes in which the processes are the fundamental aspects of successful project management. In fact, project managers strive to find the best way to streamline processes in such a way that people can become interchangeable and replaceable.

Under these circumstances, people play a secondary role. This mentality is a reflection on the overall mentality of the management team in running things. This is why Agile implies a fundamental shift from processes and embraces people at all levels.

Furthermore, traditional project management methodologies and business practices tend to be rigid and afford little room for innovation and creativity. This was the largest driving force behind the creation of the so-called "Agile Manifesto".

This manifesto is a declaration made by some of the top software developers of their time in order to formally adopt a much more flexible and innovative project management framework. As such, the Agile Manifesto became the basis for the conceptual framework that would provide the underlying philosophy for the Scrum and other Agile project management methodologies.

In 2001, these developers produced the Agile manifesto, which reads as follows:

We are uncovering better ways of developing software by doing it and helping others do it. Through this work we have come to value:

- Individuals and interactions over processes and tools
- Working software over comprehensive documentation
- Customer collaboration over contract negotiation
- Responding to change over following a plan

That is, while there is value in the items on the right, we value the items on the left more.

As you can see, Agile is about people over process, collaboration over negotiations, functionality over paperwork, and change over a plan.

Under this concept, Agile easily becomes the most adaptable means of embracing change and setting yourself and your organization up for success. Agile isn't just about finding a new and creative way of doing things, but it is about finding ways of making sustainable changes which will lead to success over longer periods of time. As such, sustainability becomes one, if not, the most important factor for Agile project management methodologies.

It should be noted that when you talk about Agile and Scrum, you are talking about two similar things though they are not the same.

First, Agile is a framework that emerged in the software development industry. The reason for the emergence of Agile was the need to find a better and more flexible way of handling projects. Since traditional project management methods try to restrict the amount of freedom, software developers realized that having a restricted range of action was not conducive to being innovative.

Prior to Agile being "born," other software development approaches, such as "Extreme Programming," also known as "XP" were utilized in developing some of the most popular software packages of all time. One clear example is Windows XP which ended up becoming one of the best iterations of the Windows operating system.

Since then, Agile became the go-to project management philosophy in the software development world. However, Agile is a philosophy, framework, and approach. Consequently, it does not have all of the requisite elements needed in order to systematize the actions to be conducted as a part of carrying out a project.

So, from the Agile foundation, Scrum emerged.

Scrum is a methodology in the sense that it contains all of the necessary procedural aspects that can lead a team to produce outputs based on the Agile framework. It should be noted that Scrum is not the only Agile-based project management methodology out there. For example, other methodologies include Feature Driven Development (FDD), Dynamic Systems Development Method (DSDM), and Adaptive Software Development (ASD) to name a few.

While we won't be discussing other Agile-based methodologies in this book, it is worth noting that the Agile manifesto has spawned a lot of methodologies which aim to harness the philosophical underpinnings that have made Agile one of the most successful approaches of all time.

However, there's a catch. The overwhelming majority of these project management methodologies are oriented toward software development. This is where Scrum becomes a much more useful methodology in as much as it provides a cross-cutting appeal.

As we will see throughout this book, Scrum's fundamental

procedures can be easily applied across any number of industries fields and areas in which change is constant and volatility tends to be the norm.

So, let's drill down and focus on how Scrum can be used to manage projects in an efficient manner in such a way that sustainable success and development are the main driving forces behind the outputs achieved as a result of teamwork and collaboration.

Basics of Scrum

A t this point, you might be asking yourself, "what exactly is Scrum?"

We have established that Scrum is a project management methodology which embraces change rather than avoiding it. In addition, we have established that Scrum is ideal for those projects with a high degree of uncertainty and volatility.

So, what exactly is Scrum?

The name Scrum comes for the sport Rugby.

Rugby is a team sport that promotes a high degree of teamwork and collaboration. In case you are not familiar with this sport, I would encourage you to check out some highlights. You will see that all players need to support each other in order for the team to be successful.

In Rugby, all players must contribute. It is not like other sports where one player can dominate while the others play a supporting cast around them. In Rugby, one player that tries to take over will end up being pounded by the opposition. That is why Rugby is a highly collaborative sport.

Consequently, the name "Scrum" is derived from the interaction and gameplay that takes place in a Rugby match.

As far as Scrum in terms of project management, it is an Agile-based methodology. This means that Scrum is intended to serve as a means of organizing and coordinating the actions among all participants in a project.

In this chapter, we will look at the three basic personas in a Scrum-based project and that various stages of a Scrum project. Moreover, we expect that you will get a firm grasp on the underpinnings that support Scrum as a methodology.

Scrum can be defined as follows: Scrum is a project management methodology that values simplicity and is based on empiricism. It follows a set of guidelines and promotes the self-organization of teams.

This last point is important as self-organizing teams are a key factor in the production of outputs. When a team is able to organize itself efficiently, then the outputs that result from this approach are the result of the collective effort as opposed to having a long and drawn out process as seen in traditional approaches.

Scrum has three important characteristics which differentiate it from its core, Agile:

- It is lightweight
- It is also simple to understand
- It is tough to master

These three points place emphasis on the fact that running a project based on Scrum requires minimal amounts of paperwork and stresses developing a collaborative nature among team members and the customer.

It is also simple to understand as there are no complex rules and procedures which must be memorized in order to understand the nuances of this approach. In fact, the average individual can get a solid understanding of Scrum within a few hours of reading and learning about it. What makes it tough is that attaining true Scrum mastery takes time. This is the case since becoming an expert Scrum practitioner takes a lot of time and effort. But, when you are able to truly master it, your outputs will be sustainable and able to withstand the test of time.

Considering that we have defined what Scrum is, it is worth discussing what Scrum is not.

Scrum is not some magic formula that will solve all of the

problems associated with running a project or getting stuff done.

Also, Scrum is not some type of predictive methodology that is based on an algorithm which can determine what you need to do at any step of the process.

So, if you believe that Scrum is some type of be all and all of things, then you need focus more on what needs to be done, timeframe, and the degree of quality with which it needs to be done as opposed to cutting corners. Ultimately, if you take the time to truly master Scrum, you will find that it will enable you to get things done a lot faster and more effectively than you had previously thought possible.

The Process of Scrum

Since Scrum acts like a methodology, there is a series of steps which must be followed in order to maximize its effectiveness. As we have stressed earlier, Scrum is not rigid and it is not predictive, that is, Scrum is open and it feeds off the creativity of each individual practitioner as opposed to expecting a cookie-cutter approach.

The core of the Scrum process is called a "sprint". A sprint is the individual iteration of the Scrum process. Thus, the entire project development is broken up into successive parts in which each of these parts must produce some type of output which can then be used as a measure of "working software".

This last point is important as the concept of "working software" implies that at the end of each sprint, the project team must be able to deliver value to the customer. Now, whether that means an actual functioning piece of equipment depends on the nature of the project. Nevertheless, at the end of each sprint, the customer will be able to see the advancement in the project itself.

The number of sprints and the duration of each sprint depend on the project itself. So, it could be that one project may last one sprint, while there may be projects that last multiple sprints. It should also be noted that testing can be conducted as part of a single sprint, or multiple sprints, depending on the nature of the work being done.

Typically, each sprint lasts for four weeks. Although, this is only a rule of thumb. The length of an individual sprint depends on a number of factors. But, in general, four weeks is a good number. It should be noted that one-week sprints may not provide you with enough time to complete tasks while sprints longer than four weeks may drag the project on needlessly.

Each sprint begins with what is known as a "Sprint Planning Meeting". The Sprint Planning Meeting consists of determining the objectives for the sprint which is about to start. Given the collaborative nature of Scrum, the objectives, or user stories to be covered will be decided by the team itself. Since the team is self-organizing, the decision of what work to be done is not dictated by the project leadership, rather, the team will decide what they want to do based on any number of factors such as time constraints, the logical progression of the work begin carried out, or the team's understanding of the project's requirements.

Once the work to be done has been decided at the Sprint Planning Meeting, the team will begin working. Every day, the team will engage in what is known as the Daily Standup Meeting. This meeting consists of having a short meeting, about 15 minutes in length, in which the issues affecting the Development Team are brought up. This could be anything related to the work being done such as issues dealing with equipment, perhaps a lack of clarity on the tasks being done, or a team member asking for help.

The Daily Standup Meeting is intended to foster communication and ensure that the Development Team can communicate with the Scrum Master in order to keep the project moving along. This meeting is very much informal in nature. However, this does not mean that it is not serious. Far from it; the matters discussed in this meeting are quite serious.

Upon the completion of the sprint, the Sprint Review Meeting takes place. At the Sprint Review Meeting, the Development Team presents the outputs of that sprint to the customer. The customer is then able to see where the project is headed and how the team has been able to meet the acceptance criteria established as the measure of success for the project.

Once the customer has given their blessing on the outputs, and potential feedback, then the Development Team moves into what is called the Sprint Retrospect Meeting. The Sprint Retrospect Meeting consists of a debrief that the Development Team engages in, in order to discuss what went right, what needs to be improved, and what issues they encountered throughout the sprint.

The Sprint Retrospect Meeting can also segue into the Sprint Planning Meeting. In this transition, the Development Team can discuss any change requests from the customer. As we will discuss later on, it's important to note that change request from customers should be addressed at the beginning of a new sprint so as to avoid altering the planning for the sprint currently in progress.

The process of Sprint Planning Meeting, sprint, Sprint Review Meeting, and Sprint Retrospect Meeting is called "iteration". This cycle is repeated as many times as needed in order to complete user stories. Once all user stories are completed and the product is fully functional, then the project can be considered to be over.

User stories

In short, user stories are a characterization of the end users of the product being developed. Now, user stories do not refer to the customer per se. The customer is the person who is commissioning the project though they may not be the one who is paying for the project. The customer is the person who is motivated to have the project happen.

In the case of user stories, these are the folks who will be using the actual product. For instance, the customer is an electronics company which has asked the project team to develop a new set of earphones. The user stories will be the customer's customers; the folks who will visit a shop and purchase the earphones.

As such, the user stories must be in line with who the end users are and why they would be motivated to purchase the product.

Consider the example of the earphones: Jim is a 25-year-old young professional. He commutes to work every day. He has a 45-minute train ride in which he likes to listen to audio-books in order to improve his skills. However, the train is very noisy, and he can't listen very well. He has tried several types of earphones and headphones, but nothing really seems to work. Noise canceling headphones are expensive and bulky. He would like a smaller, cost-effective option which can help him when he's on-the-go.

In this example, we have given the end user a name and a face. In doing so, the Development Team is not looking to develop this product for a "customer", but for "Jim". They know who he is, and how he looks like (yes, you can find a real picture of a person whom you envision your end user would be like). This visual enables the team to focus on a real person. Ultimately, this visual input provides something tangible on which the Development Team can channel their efforts.

Since a project may have multiple user stories, the project cannot be deemed as completed until all user stories have been covered. It should be said that there is no need to develop individual products to address each user story, but rather, certain features of a single product may address individual user stories.

The Roles in Scrum

Also, there are roles to be played in Scrum.

There are three major roles in Scrum: the Product Owner, the Scrum, and the Development Team. Each one plays a specific role within the team and none has authority over the other(s). Scrum requires a flat structure. Therefore, one team member cannot expect to have control over the others.

In the case of the Product Owner, this is the "voice of the customer," meaning that the Product Owner will be in constant communication with the customer and to relay this information to the Scrum Master and Development Team. Generally, the Product Owner will communicate with the Scrum Master and then the Scrum Master will incorporate any additional information to the Development Team. The Product Owner is generally the first player on the team and will most likely be in charge of selecting the Scrum Master and the Development Team.

The Scrum Master is known as a "subservient leader". The Scrum Master is intended to act as coordinator in order to ensure that all activities are running smoothly and that the Development Team has all the tools they need in order to do their job. This implies that the Scrum Master will be working very closely with the Development Team in order to address issues as they come up. In addition, the Scrum Master must develop a good sense for dealing with issues proactively before they become any type of serious hindrance to the project's development.

As for the Development Team, these are the individuals who are actually in charge of creating the product that the project aims to develop. They are skilled in their craft and are more than likely specialists in their field. They may have some limited knowledge and experience in Scrum, whereas, the Scrum Master and the Product Owner must be very well-versed in Scrum methodology.

The Development Team is in charge of deciding what work will be done and when it will be done. This is what happens at the Sprint Planning Meeting. The ultimate decision of what to include and what not to include is the result of the discussion among the Scrum Master and the Development Team.

Finally, the Development Team generally consists of 4 to 8

members. Any team larger than 10 members should be broken up into two smaller groups, or perhaps subgroups, in order to facilitate communication and coordination among them. This is why transparent communication and collaboration are two of the foundational pillars of a successful Scrum team.

2

The Sprint

In the previous chapter, we touched upon the generalities of a sprint. A sprint, as we have previously indicated, is the iteration of the Scrum process. As such, each sprint is a way in which the process of conducting a Scrum-based project is broken down into manageable bits with the intent of producing a specific deliverable.

Consequently, each sprint seeks to divide the sum of the project's output into individual phases in such a way that the project team is able to meet project deliverables within the allotted timeframe.

So, we will take a closer look at what a sprint is and how it is organized in order to achieve the sprint's objectives as a means of attaining the project's final outcomes.

What is a Sprint?

Previously, we established that a sprint is an iteration of the Scrum methodology. As such, a sprint is the way in which the Development Team is able to successfully complete the user stories as outlined at the beginning of the project.

A project typically begins with a project sponsor. The project sponsor is the person who is interested in making the project happen. Now, the project sponsor could also be the customer, that is, the person who is essentially paying for the project. In any event, the project sponsor and the customer are considered stakeholders in the project, that is, they have some type of interest in making the project happen.

In addition, anyone else who has any kind of interest or stake in the project will also be considered a stakeholder. This is important to note as there may be multiple parties who are interested in seeing the project through. However, the Scrum Master and the Development Team will have no relation with these stakeholders. The liaison between the Development Team and any interested stakeholders is the Product Owner.

As previously stated, the Product Owner is the individual who is known as "the voice of the customer". In this regard, the Development Team will receive feedback and guidance from the customer through the Product Owner in order to ensure that they have taken the customer's feedback and requirements into account.

Once the customer and stakeholders have given the green light for the project to get underway, the customer needs to find a "project manager" to take charge and get the project off the ground. Under traditional project management methodologies, the project manager is the individual who is the "boss" of the project.

Under this scenario, the project manager is in charge of assembling the project team and making sure that the project gets completed according to the specifications made by the customer. However, Scrum tends to be a bit different in the sense that the Product Owner is not the "boss" of the project. Rather, the Product Owner is the main coordinator who is in charge of articulating the customer's vision into a language which is understandable by the project team.

One of the Product Owner's most important tasks is to find the right Scrum Master. Considering that the Product Owner is generally well-versed in Scrum methodology, the Scrum Master also needs to be adept in the ways of Agile and Scrum.

In this regard, the Product Owner and the Scrum Master can work in tandem to choose their Development Team. The Development Team is in charge of actually producing the value to the customer. So, the Development Team needs to be comprised of individuals who are not only adept in the actual discipline in which they are expected to produce but also have some type of understanding in the ways of Scrum.

At this point, the newly formed Scrum team is ready to begin the planning phase of the project. As such, the project's final product needs to be determined. Often, the project's final product will be determined by the customer. The customer may indicate that they want to build a car, run a marketing campaign or produce software.

Other times, the customer may indicate the solution they want but not necessarily the actual product. For instance, the customer may indicate that they need an app to help their customers, increase their sales, or improve their service. In this case, the project team will come up with the actual product that will serve the customer's needs.

In addition, the project team, as a whole, may develop the user stories that will make up the target audience that will benefit from the project's final output. In some cases though, the Product Owner will work with the customer in order to develop the user stories. Nevertheless, the Product Owner and the Scrum Master may work with the Development Team especially when they are unfamiliar with the technology that is behind the solution they are aiming to provide.

With user stories crafted and ready to go, the Development Team can sit down and begin to produce what is known as the Product Backlog. The Product Backlog essentially consists of the various tasks that will need to be completed in order for the project to come to fruition.

The Product Backlog is groomed after each sprint as the Development Team continues to complete each user story. It should be noted that a project may have several user stories and thereby have an extensive Product Backlog.

In other cases, a short project may have just the one user story, and therefore, a shorter Product Backlog. When the entire Product Backlog is set up, the Scrum team can then proceed to create the Sprint Backlog at each Sprint Planning Meeting.

Now that the Scrum team is ready to run their first sprint, it should be said that the Development Team does not necessarily need to be physically located in the same place. While co-location is a big deal in a sprint, that is, having the Development Team all together in a single spot, it's worth mentioning that the Development Team may be able to work remotely depending on the scope of the project and the deliverables in a given sprint. It could be that the Development Team may not need to be physically located in every sprint, but there should come a point where the team needs to be together in one place.

Given the right project, the entire Scrum team could work remotely. This would be possible if the project's scope and ultimate deliverables don't actually consist in a physical item. This is possible with project's that aim to produce software or some other intangible good such as a marketing campaign or even a product design. Whatever the case, the project may afford a greater degree of flexibility in terms of what the final output will be.

The Daily Standup Meeting

At the beginning of each working day, the Development Team will meet with the Scrum Master and hold what is known as the Daily Standup Meeting. This meeting consists of a short meeting, typically 15 minutes in length, in which the Development Team has the chance to discuss how the project is going, what challenges they are facing, and what issues they have solved as a result.

The Scrum Master also has the opportunity to learn more about what the team is doing and how this can affect their overall performance. In that regard, the Development Team has the opportunity to coordinate with the Scrum Master in order to obtain resources, such as equipment, which might be needed in order to complete a given user story.

The Daily Standup Meeting also serves as an opportunity for the team to come closer together as a unit given their working relationship. Even if the team is working remotely, the Daily Standup Meeting can serve as a means of checking in with another and keep track of the project's progress.

Keeping Track of Progress

Another important element in each sprint pertains to tracking progress.

In a typical sprint, there are two main ways in which the Development Team can keep track of the sprint's progress.

The first tool is known as the Sprint Backlog. The Sprint Backlog consists of the tasks that were decided upon at the Sprint Planning Meeting. These tasks are "cleared" upon their completion. In general, the Scrum Master is in charge of ensuring that the completed user stories, or tasks in the Sprint Backlog, are updated accordingly.

Failure to track progress can lead the Scrum team to lose focus and potentially miss deadlines. If the Scrum team runs into unexpected issues, they can always find a way to deal with it, or leave tasks for the following sprint.

The second tool used to track progress is the Burndown Chart. The Burndown Chart is used to keep track of the time remaining in a sprint. As such, each day that passes gradually reduces the amount of time remaining in a sprint.

For instance, if you are working 8 hours a day for a 4-week period, you are talking about a total of 160 hours over the course of a sprint. This means that each working day is reduced by 8 hours until it eventually reaches zero on the final day of the sprint.

Now, it could be that the Development Team is forced to put in some overtime. In that case, those overtime hours are tracked and compared to the project's overall progress. Ultimately, the Scrum team may end up working more than 160 hours in that specific sprint. This is an important measure as it serves to gauge how efficiently the Scrum team is using its time.

Consequently, tracking progress effectively will enable to project team to better manage their time and gauge how effective their work has actually been.

Feedback at the End of a Sprint

At the end of each sprint, the customer has the opportunity to see what the Development Team has been able to produce. This demonstration typically happens at the Sprint Review Meeting. In this meeting, the Development Team may have some "working software" to display to the customer. In other cases, a working prototype may not be feasible yet.

Then, there are projects which do not yield working prototypes. In any event, the Development Team must show value to the customer at the end of each sprint. This is an important part of the Scrum methodology as the Sprint Review Meeting enables the Scrum team to receive feedback from the customer and other project stakeholders.

It is very important for the Scrum team to take feedback in

stride as it is the basis for delivering what the customer truly needs and wants, in addition to delivering value at all stages of the project. Furthermore, feedback can also be the basis for change management. As such, managing change management is a fundamental part of effective sprint management.

3

Sprint Planning Meeting, Sprint Review, and Sprint Retrospect

I n the previous chapter, we had an overview of what a sprint is and the components that comprise it. Given that a sprint makes up one part of the entire Scrum project, the Development Team needs to have a clear understanding of how to plan each sprint effectively.

By managing to plan each sprint effectively, the Scrum team can handle the project's requirements and deliver the project's output according to the deadline. Consequently, the team needs to gain a keen understanding of the following meetings:

1. The Sprint Planning Meeting
2. The Sprint Review Meeting
3. The Sprint Retrospect Meeting

These three different meetings, which happen at various stages of the project, enable the Scrum team to produce the outputs that are required as a part of the project. As such, the Scrum team needs to take advantage of each meeting in order to plan work effectively for the following sprint.

So, let's drill down into what each of the above-mentioned meetings entails.

The Sprint Planning Meeting

We have discussed the Sprint Planning Meeting at earlier points in this book.

The first Sprint Planning Meeting takes place right after the Development Team has been assembled and the Product Backlog has been built.

At the first Sprint Planning Meeting, the Development Team will determine which tasks ought to be the first in the queue. What this implies is that the Development Team needs to figure out which user stories and which tasks require immediate attention.

This is where it gets tricky.

The Development Team may decide to tackle the most important tasks first. As such, the most important tasks may be due to the fact that these are tasks which serve as the foundation for the rest of the tasks in the Product Backlog.

In other cases, the Development Team may choose to get through the easiest, or the hardest, tasks first and then focus on the remaining tasks which may demand more, or less, attention. Under these circumstances, the Development Team has the option to decide what they will work on based on the number of sprints they have available and the amount of work to be completed.

It should be noted that the number of sprints does not depend on the Development Team. While there might be cases in which the Scrum team decides how long a project will take, most of the time, the project doesn't have much of a choice. For example, they may only have four weeks to complete a given project time and/or budgetary constraints. In such cases, the Development Team needs to make the number of sprints available work with the number of tasks to be completed.

After the initial Sprint Planning Meeting, the Development Team will get to work on the first sprint until its completion. Subsequently, Sprint Planning Meetings will depend on the output of the previous sprint and the feedback received from the customer.

In addition, there may be change requests from the customer. So, these elements need to be taken into account when engaging upon the next sprint's Sprint Planning Meeting.

Regarding change management, it's crucial to note that changes should not be introduced mid-sprint. When changes are introduced mid-sprint, the Development Team's rhythm may be upset and lead the team to lose focus. Moreover, the time taken to plan the sprint may end up being useless if the Scrum Master and/or the Product Owner agree to change setting at mid-sprint.

If things change so drastically, especially due to unforeseen conditions, it might be best to cancel the sprint and start over. Now, canceling a sprint is not the most advisable thing to do, the Scrum Master and the Product Owner may consider doing so in order to avoid useless work and get the project back on track.

One other thing: the Sprint Planning Meeting must be attended by the entire Development Team and the Scrum Master. They will sit down and go over what must be done in the upcoming sprint. This meeting can be held at any time, though it would probably be best to hold it on a Monday morning right at the outset of the new sprint. That way, the Development Team and the Scrum Master will have the rest of the week ahead of them to begin the new sprint.

The Product Owner may choose to attend the Sprint Planning Meeting thought it is not necessary. The Product Owner may choose to attend especially when there have been change requests on the part of the customer. Otherwise, the Product Owner may choose to forego the Sprint Planning Meeting, though the Product Owner may request to meet with the Scrum team with the intent of gathering information to update the customer.

The Sprint Review Meeting

At the end of the sprint, the sprint's outcomes are presented to the customer at the Sprint Review Meeting.

The purpose of this meeting is in line with one of the principles of Agile which is to deliver value to the customer even at early stages in the development of the project. As such, the Sprint Review Meeting is intended to present the project team's advances in order for the customer to see how the project is coming along.

The Sprint Review Meeting can be as simple, or as elaborate, as the project team sees fit. For instance, it might be a formal event in which an early prototype might be unveiled. In other cases, the Sprint Review Meeting may be a test run of the product. In such cases, the customer has the opportunity to test out the product and provide their feedback. However, when the team chooses to hold the Sprint Review Meeting, the main objective is to demonstrate that the project has progressively achieved its objectives.

At the Sprint Review Meeting, the entire Scrum team should be present in addition to the customer and all project stakeholders. This implies that the Sprint Review Meeting aims to achieve cohesion among all of the actors involved in the project.

Now, the feedback provided by the customer at the Sprint Review Meeting is of the utmost importance.

In some cases, the customer might be thrilled and not provide any significant feedback. In such cases, the customer's blessing serves as a means of motivating the team to move forward and provide guidance for the upcoming sprint.

In other cases, the customer may provide feedback on the features and elements that make up the final product. This feedback may be related to simple aspects such as layout, color, and other visual aspects of the product, while feedback may also refer to more profound aspects such as the solution it actually provides to the end user.

Also, the Sprint Review Meeting provides an opportunity for the customer to present change requests. These change requests may not be related to the actual work of the Scrum team, that is, the customer requesting changes based on ineffectiveness on the part of the Scrum team. Rather, it could be that the customer has realized they want additional features or functionalities. Furthermore, the customer may choose to change their mind on specific features thus requesting changes.

If, and when, the customer chooses to make a change

request, the Product Owner is the one who needs to translate this change request into the type of language which the Development Team can understand and turn into actions that reflect the change request on the part of the customer.

The Sprint Retrospect Meeting

At the end of the sprint, the final phase that takes place is the Sprint Retrospect Meeting. This meeting is intended to give the Scrum team the opportunity to debrief and reflect on the past sprint's successes and shortcomings. As a result, the Scrum team will be able to analyze what they feel needs to be improved while making sure that the good trends continue.

This meeting also provides the opportunity for team members to address issues and challenges which they have been facing throughout the sprint and the project. For example, there might be a gap in the technical knowledge of the team. As such, the team may choose to bring in an expert who can support them such as an Agile Coach.

In this specific example, an Agile Coach is an expert in Agile and Scrum methodology. This Coach will help guide the Scrum team in learning the finer points of the Scrum methodology while ensuring its correct application throughout the various tasks and sprints.

Furthermore, the Scrum team may find it important to address issues that may potentially come up and deal with them in a proactive manner. Consequently, the Scrum team may choose to find the necessary elements that will enable them to deal with such issues before they become a problem.

The Sprint Retrospect Meeting may also serve as a springboard into the Sprint Planning Meeting. The reason for this is that customer feedback is also discussed at the Sprint Retrospect Meeting. Thus, the Scrum team has the opportunity to discuss the customer's feedback and incorporate it into the upcoming sprint. This would provide a logical segue into the next sprint.

By the same token, the Sprint Retrospect Meeting can also deal with change requests from the customer as a result of their feedback following the Sprint Review Meeting. Also, the customer may have made a change request at some point during the sprint. Since the Scrum team does not incorporate changes mid-sprint, the Product Owner may choose the Sprint Retrospect Meeting as the opportunity to bring up the matter and then transition into the Sprint Planning Meeting so that the matter can be discussed and then integrated into the Sprint Backlog in the next sprint.

Finally, it's worth mentioning that the Sprint Retrospect Meeting doesn't have to be a boring affair. This can be done in a setting in which the team can relax and enjoy some time together as a team. It could be on a weekend or during a team dinner. The important thing is to have enough time to relax and discuss matters openly and honestly.

As long as the team is able to deal with things openly and maturely, there will always be positive outcomes at the Sprint Retrospect Meeting. Hopefully, both the positives and the negatives will lead to a good Sprint Planning Meeting and a subsequent successful sprint.

4

Artifacts of Scrum

In this chapter, we are going to be taking a look at the artifacts of Scrum.

When we use the term "artifact", we are talking about tools which are used in the design and management of the Scrum project. Thus, we are talking about tools which can be used to make sense of how the project is going to be managed and run so that the project team can make the most of the overall work that needs to be done.

These artifacts are part of each, individual sprint. As such, being able to use these artifacts appropriately will enable the Scrum team to effectively produce the outputs to the best of their abilities. Consequently, the artifact that will be described in this chapter is not so much about the output themselves, but rather, understanding what the project requires.

So, let's jump in and a have a closer look at how these artifacts apply to in the running of an average sprint.

Sustainable Pace

One of the core Agile principles is maintaining a sustainable pace.

When we discuss a sustainable pace, it's important that this refers to being able to maintain a tempo that the entire Development Team can keep throughout the entire project. It is crucial for the project team to make sure they are able to work at a pace which they can logically follow as keeping a steady pace will help the Development Team stay on track and meet their deadlines.

When a Development Team is able to maintain a sustainable pace, it makes it easier to predict where the project will be headed and how the Scrum team can get there. The most important thing to bear in mind is that the Scrum team has the opportunity to make the most of their time especially in light of the Burndown chart.

The drawback of working at an unsustainable pace is that the Scrum team may end up working at a tempo which will lead the team to burnout at some point. What this leads to is an unfortunate outcome since the Scrum team may end up becoming unable to meet the project's objectives within the allotted timeframe.

For inexperience Scrum Masters, it is quite easy to fall into this trap and let the team work at an unsustainable pace. If that were the case, then the entire project's outcomes would be in jeopardy. It goes without saying that if the Development Team should end up working at an unsustainable pace for extended periods of time, the potential for the law of diminishing returns to kick in is great. If such a thing were possible, then it may lead the entire team to become less productive, thus risking the overall quality of the project's final products.

Hence, ensuring a sustainable pace throughout the lifecycle of the project is vital in as much as allowing the Scrum team to produce what is meant to be produced within the project's deadlines.

The Product Backlog

As stated earlier, the Product Backlog refers to the number of tasks which need to be completed as a part of the overall production of the project's output.

The Product Backlog should not be seen as a checklist or a To-do list. Rather, it should be seen as the individual components that make up the entire project's output.

For instance, if the project is meant to produce a new electric passenger vehicle, the Scrum team may break up the production of this output into manageable chunks based on the user stories (more on that in a bit).

So, the Development Team considers that, in the overall scheme of things, the most important step is to come up with a functional design. Now, the design in itself may not necessarily be the project's output, but it could be the deliverable at the end of a sprint. Consequently, the Development Team will work at producing the design for the new electric vehicle at the end of that sprint.

The Product Backlog is built around the project's final outcome and is then broken down into the individual sprints for that individual project. So, if the project has contemplated 10 sprints, the Product Backlog would then be divided up over the 10 sprints.

Does that mean that the Product Backlog should be divided up into 10 equal parts?

Not necessarily.

Given the dynamic nature of Scrum, one sprint may address a fairly limited number of items in the Product Backlog while another sprint may address a greater number. At the end of the day, it all depends on what is to be covered in that given sprint in light of the project's final outcome.

Grooming the Product Backlog

It is generally the Scrum Master's responsibility to groom the Product Backlog.

What does this mean?

It means that the Scrum Master should keep track of the completed items contained in the Product Backlog. This is what grooming is all about.

The main reason behind grooming the Product Backlog is so that the team knows where it stands and doesn't end up doing tasks twice or miss the completion of other tasks in the backlog.

As such, one of the dangers that a Scrum team may face if they are unable to have a clear Product Backlog is missing vital tasks in the project's Product Backlog. That, in addition to incomplete tasks, may lead the team to fall behind or simply make mistakes in the development of the project. Needless to say, missing product components and features would be a disastrous outcome in the overall scope of the project.

Sprint Backlog

Once the Scrum team has devised the project's Product Backlog, the Scrum team then needs to come up with the Sprint Backlog at the Sprint Planning Meeting. In the Sprint

Planning Meeting, the Scrum team will determine which of the tasks contained in the Product Backlog will be completed in that particular sprint.

As such, the Scrum team needs to determine which of the items in the Product Backlog need to be dealt with first before moving on to the following items.

Earlier, we discussed some of the criteria that go into selecting which items will go into the Sprint Backlog. In general, this refers to ensuring a logical progression in the project's completion. This is especially true when the items in the Product Backlog are interdependent in such a way that one item depends on the completion of another. That is, the team cannot start working on one item until another item has been completed first.

This interdependency is vital for the overall completion of the project as tasks may get held up due to the lack of completion of previous ones.

One caveat in the Sprint Backlog is that the Scrum team must determine which items may be feasibly completed during that time. So, the team must ensure that whatever is included can be completed within the timeframe of the sprint. If an item requires multiple sprints before it is completed, then the Scrum team must determine how many sprints it would take to complete and consequently break down the item into manageable chunks.

As with the Product Backlog, the Scrum Master ought to be

the one in charge of making sure that it is updated. Although, any member of the Scrum team could keep track of the grooming of the Sprint Backlog. Nevertheless, it should be noted that it's best if the Scrum Master handled this task as the Development Team is best suited for the actual development of the project and not an administrative task which would be easily handled by the Scrum Master.

The Burndown Chart

Earlier we touched on the Burndown Chart albeit briefly.

The Product Burndown Chart refers to the amount of time the entire project has to develop the final output for the project.

In this case, the Project Burndown Chart can be broken down into the individual sprints that have been decided for the project.

Now, deciding on the number of sprints for an individual project depends on the overall time the Scrum team has to complete the project. So, some projects may have more, or less, time available for its completion. In other cases, the project may have a very tight turnaround. Therefore, the Scrum team needs to work as fast as possible. In other occasions, the Scrum team may have a project which is rather simple and straightforward. As such, they may not need a great deal of time to get it done.

Regardless of the time available, the number of sprints can be as broad as required. For the sake of simplicity, let's assume that project X has been broken down into three, four-week sprints. That means that the project has a total of 12 weeks to be completed.

So, the Project Burndown Chart would have three blocks corresponding to each sprint. Thus, the Product Burndown Chart will visualize the entire block of time as broken down into each sprint. Assuming that the team is working 5 days a week, that provides a total of 60 working days. Each day can also be broken down into 8-hour segments. So, the project would have a total of 480 hours to be completed. Hence, the Project Burndown Chart would be able to track the entire project's time allotted for its completion.

Both the Development Team and the Scrum Master can keep an eye on the time remaining on the project and adjust their sprint planning accordingly.

Sprint Burndown Chart

The Sprint Burndown Chart works exactly the same way the Product Burndown Chart does. The difference is that the Sprint Burndown Chart visualizes the amount of time available to the individual sprint regardless of the overall amount of time available to the project itself.

Hence, the Development Team can see how much time they

have left to complete the items in the Sprint Backlog and compare their pace. This can help the team adjust their tempo in order to maintain a sustainable pace across the sprint, or the project itself.

It should be said that if the Development Team is running ahead of schedule, the "extra" time leftover should be allotted to testing in such a way that the team has the opportunity to make sure that the products and outputs are being developed according to customer specifications and acceptance criteria.

User Stories

Considering that we have discussed user stories at a considerable length in earlier chapters, it's worth mentioning at this point that the user stories which have been developed for a given project should provide the guidelines which the Scrum team needs in order to make the product work.

As such, the Development Team needs to keep track of the completion of user stories so that there is clarity in the work that has already been completed. Therefore, it is up to the Scrum Master to make sure that user stories are up to date so that the Scrum team is on the same page and focused on the work to be done.

Ultimately, both the Scrum Master and the Development Team should be well aware of the progress made on individual user stories and what needs to be done in order to complete them. This is especially true if the completion of a user story spans more than one sprint.

5

The Scrum Master as a
Subservient Leader

Throughout this book, we have talked about the Scrum Master within the development of the project. In this chapter, we will focus on the leadership within a Scrum project and the role that the Product Owner and the Scrum Master play within the project itself.

First of all, it is important to point out the fact that leadership in a Scrum project is just that, leadership. As such, leadership is not about being the "boss" or being "in charge". Since Scrum advocates a flat organizational structure, the main focus is on getting things done as opposed to following procedures and ensuring a proper chain of command.

This is one of the most important differences between Agile methodologies and traditional project management methodologies. In a traditional context, leaders are in charge of making sure that tasks get done regardless of who is actually doing the work.

So, let's drill down and focus on the roles played by the Product Owner and the Scrum Master within the realization of a Scrum-based project.

The Role of the Product Owner

Earlier, we defined the Product Owner as the voice of the customer". This role as the "voice of the customer" means that the Product Owner will become the liaison between the Scrum team and the customer.

This is a very important leadership that comes with no functional authority. So, this means that the Product Owner is not in a position to dictate the work that is to be done or which tasks are to be completed in a sprint.

Generally speaking, the Product Owner takes on the role of "project manager". However, the traditional role of a project manager is to be the individual who is responsible for the project's outcomes. This creates a single point of accountability and also a single point of authority.

Thus, traditional project management considers a hierarchical structure as the best means in order to run projects. Based on that assumption, the project manager uses their functional authority in order to ensure the project is run in accordance with the overall scope of activities.

That being said, Scrum-based projects do not require such functionality and authority over anyone. In fact, the role of the Product Owner becomes one in which the Development Team comes to rely on the Scrum Master to relay information over to the Product Owner so that the Product Owner can coordinate with the customer.

So, the Product Owner, while playing a key leadership role within the Scrum team, works behind the scenes in order to ensure that the Scrum team has everything it needs to become fully functional and operational.

One very important note about the Product Owner's profile: the Product Owner, as such, should be well-versed in the ways of Scrum and Agile, though the Product Owner may not necessarily be an expert in the project field. Nevertheless, the Product Owner must have a solid understanding of the final product since it is up to the Product Owner to translate the customer's vision into the language which the Development Team will understand.

As a result, the Product Owner will become a referent in terms of Scrum methodology but not in terms of how the Development Team will approach the development of the project's final solution.

The Role of the Scrum Master

The Scrum Master has a unique role within the project management world.

Most project coordinators have some type of functional authority over the project team. As a coordinator, their role is to make sure that everyone is doing what they are supposed to be doing when they are supposed to be doing it. Consequently, the project coordinator has a more disciplinary role since it is up to the project coordinator to make sure that things run smoothly.

However, Scrum puts a completely different spin on the role of project coordinator. So, the Scrum Master acts as a project coordinator but without the functional authority. What that implies is that the Scrum Master is dedicated to ensuring that the project itself is running smoothly, but from a perspective of supporting the Development Team.

This support implies that the Scrum Master must be constantly vigilant in tracking what the Development Team needs, the challenges they might be facing, and any other potential headwinds the Development Team may encounter.

Furthermore, the Scrum Master should be wel' Scrum methodology. As such, the Scrum Ma focused on making sure that the Scrum m being implemented in the correct manner. V

Master may not necessarily be the definitive judge in all matters pertaining to methodology, the Scrum Master should act as a referee, most of the time, when questions and uncertainty regarding Scrum methodology arise.

In addition, the Scrum Master, as a "subservient leader," is in charge of liaising between the team and the Product Owner. The reason for this chain of communication is to alleviate the Development Team from any distractions. Thus, having to communicate back and forth may end up taking away from the Development Team's attention.

Consequently, having the Scrum Master and the Product Owner both communicating among themselves and the customer, reduces the need for the Development Team to take on any tasks which are not related to their own tasks within the actual development of the project.

Since Scrum has a flat organizational structure, communication among the Development Team, Scrum Master and the Product Owner should be on a peer-to-peer level. This means that there is no hierarchical structure to speak of. The fact that there are different interlocutors throughout the development process means that the Development Team can focus solely on coming up with the project's final deliverables. The Scrum Master then sits in the background taking care of any issues, preferably in a proactive manner, so that the Development Team is at liberty to handle anything they might need.

Finally, the Scrum Master should have a very good working knowledge of the project's subject area. While the Scrum Master may not be on the same level as the Development Team, the Scrum Master should have a clear understanding of the solution that is being developed. This will enable the Scrum Master to support the Development Team in case there are any technical issues. Moreover, the Scrum Master's understanding of the subject matter will enable the Scrum Master to ensure that things are on the right track.

Agile Coach

One non-member of the Scrum team, but who may emerge at some point, is the Agile Coach.

An Agile Coach is a subject matter expert in Agile and Scrum methodology. This coach may be brought at some point when there are questions or uncertainty about how Scrum methodology should be implemented. This implies that the Agile Coach will, essentially, coach the entire Scrum team on how the project should be conducted under the Agile and Scrum umbrella.

Agile coaches are generally brought in when Scrum teams are inexperienced or when an organization is going through a transformation and is beginning to implement Scrum methodology. Given the fact the Agile Coach is not a member of the Scrum team, they must have an impartial, third-party perspective on the issues and matters that go on with the Scrum team.

Therefore, the Scrum team may count on the Agile Coach for portions of the project or even throughout the entire life of the project. Sometimes, organizations will bring in Agile coaches to address very specific issues or provide in-service training to the Scrum team.

Other uses for an Agile Coach may include providing training to the Scrum team especially when an organization is running a Scrum-based project for the first time. It should be noted that the Scrum team will not count on the Agile Coach for any support pertaining to the development of the actual project, nor will the Agile Coach have any influence whatsoever in how the project is run, or what tasks are done as a part of the project.

So, the Agile Coach will just accompany the project team in their endeavors, though the Agile Coach will never have any direct influence over the way the project is conducted. Nevertheless, the Agile Coach will most likely share their experience in developing projects so that the Scrum team can get a sense of how they can approach their tasks.

If an organization warrants it, the Agile Coach may even support the Product Owner in the selection of a Scrum Master and integration of the Development Team. Therefore, the Agile Coach may play a pivotal role in the organization of the project, though the ultimate decisions are up to the Scrum team.

The Agile Coach is usually brought in by the project sponsors or relevant stakeholders, though the Scrum Master or Product Owner may bring up the issue and need for the Agile Coach and bring them in themselves. At the end of the day, the Agile Coach will provide the guidance the team needs based on their particular characteristics, both team-wise and project-wise.

6

Making the Transition to Scrum

Earlier in this book, we talked about adopting the Agile mindset. In short, the Agile mindset is about embracing the concepts presented in the Agile manifesto in such a way that you, and your organization, can move toward a more flexible and dynamic approach, not just to project management, but to the overall underlying philosophy in your organization.

For some organizations, it's hard to move away from a traditional, hierarchical approach to project management and overall business management to a flat organizational structure in which the usual roles of authority and supervision and sent by the wayside.

Under that approach, project teams are subordinate to the authority of the project manager and other individuals who have functional authority. This implies that coordination is based on "taking orders" while the tasks are to be done as per instructions provided.

This approach takes away from a team's creativity and ability to solve problems in a new and innovative manner. Often, teams become discouraged since they must follow orders even when they may have a better way of doing things. In approaching business practices, in general, under this approach, the project team will stick to following orders. This not only limits the type of outputs the project team is capable of producing but ultimately reduces the project's output to what the project manager is able to conceive.

In an approach such as this, the project manager must be an all-knowing sage who has everything under control. This implies that the project manager must be right at all times. If the project manager happens to be wrong, then the project will not work out and the results could be disastrous. As such, the project team is treated with another tool that is used to achieve the end state of the project.

Since there is very little input from the project team, the project manager is left up to decide what gets done, how it gets done, and when it gets done. This is hardly the best way of conducting business as the project manager, unless very experienced, may encounter headwinds that could potentially make the project a lot harder to complete.

While this isn't to say that the project will fail under a traditional project management approach, it does imply that subscribing to such an approach may not be the most advantageous approach especially when projects face a great deal of uncertainty.

Therefore, Agile has become a solid alternative especially in those projects which do not have a high degree of certainty. When this happens, the level of confidence in the project team may be low and fear may set in.

However, when the team is empowered to use their knowledge and expertise, the project team may very well rally together and come up with innovative solutions that cannot only address the needs or the project but also produce effective and efficient ways of doing things.

Consequently, an organization that is willing to embrace the principles of Agile may find a great way of being innovative and producing high-impact results with a fraction of the effort previously required. So, let's take a look at how the principles of Agile can help organizations become more effective and lean in their approach to project management.

- **Our highest priority is to satisfy the customer through early and continuous delivery of valuable software.**

This first principle is fairly straightforward. The aim of all Agile-based or Scrum-based projects is to deliver value to the customer at all steps of the process especially in the early stages of the project. This will enable the project team to see how things may be improved based solely on the feedback from the customer and other relevant stakeholders. It will also allow the team to assess how their work is coming along.

- **Welcome changing requirements, even late in development. Agile processes harness change for the customer's competitive advantage.**

As you can see, change is the norm under Agile. So, your organization should not be afraid of change. Rather, your organization should embrace it and make the most of the opportunities to deliver value to the customer and even find new and innovative ways of getting the job done.

- **Deliver working software frequently, from a couple of weeks to a couple of months, with a preference to the shorter timescale**.

While this principle of Agile explicitly states "software," bear in mind that we are talking about the product regardless of the field of action in which it is produced. So, whether it is a car or a spaceship, the project should be able to deliver a working solution at all stages of the project. The shorter the time that working prototypes can be produced;

the better it will be for both the customer and the project team.

- **Business people and developers must work together daily throughout the project.**

This principle underscores the fundamentally collaborative nature of Agile and Scrum. Thus, the focus of the Agile mindset is not to give orders, but rather, to provide team members with the opportunity to use their creative juices and come up with solutions and ideas which can make the end result of the project much more effective and efficient.

- **Build projects around motivated individuals. Give them the environment and support they need, and trust them to get the job done**.

In a nutshell, this is the job of the Scrum Master. The Scrum Development Team should have everything they need in order to get their job done at all time. However, it is not enough to provide them with the means, but it is also imperative that the Development Team be motivated and ready to go on a consistent basis. This motivation stems from being able to choose their own work tempo, tasks to complete, and self-organize within the team setting.

- **The most efficient and effective method of**

conveying information to and within a development team is a face-to-face conversation.

While there are many communication tools which can facilitate communication among the members of a team, ultimately, there is a clear need for face-to-face communication at some point. This type of communication allows the team to maintain a high degree of trust so that they feel comfortable among themselves at all times. Best of all, a team that is able to communicate effectively is a team that can consistently deliver on their goals.

1. **Working software is the primary measure of progress.** In short, if the product does not work, then success isn't coming. And while the principle mentions "working software", this implies any of the potential product outcomes. As such, the project team should always strive to deliver working versions of the product even if they are far from being the final product release.

2. **Agile processes promote sustainable development. The sponsors, developers, and users should be able to maintain a constant pace indefinitely.**

Agile-based projects should strive to maintain a tempo which could potentially be sustained for an unlimited amount of time. While projects are not meant to last forever, the team should find such a tempo in order to avoid burnout and maintain a high degree of readiness. By maintaining a sustainable pace, the team will be able to deliver as long as it is needed in order for the project to come to fruition. If the team works too fast, then the biggest risk is burnout. On the other hand, if the team works too slow, the momentum may be hard to develop.

- **Continuous attention to technical excellence and good design enhances agility.**

This one is a biggie in terms of achieving technical excellence in the delivery of the project's ultimate outcomes. When this happens, the project will be able to deliver quality products and solutions. Given the flexible nature of Agile and Scrum, the project team will be able to make the most out of the collaborative nature of the project team.

- **Simplicity - the art of maximizing the amount of work not done - is essential.**

In this regard, work not done is just as valuable as work actually done. So, the project team must strive to cut out unnecessary tasks as much as possible. When the project team is able to reduce the number of tasks that they will need to complete, they can pay greater attention to excellence and ensure that the final product delivered will live up to the standards of the customer.

- **The best architectures, requirements, and designs emerge from self-organizing teams.**

This is another principle that is directly correlated to the concept of self-organization and collaboration. I hope that you can see how there is a pattern emerging here. Teams that are able to work out solutions for themselves, but not being left on their own without any support, generally come up with much better solutions as compared to teams who only follow orders. So, don't be afraid to foster self-organization and collaboration. These are the most important qualities that any Scrum team can develop collectively.

- **At regular intervals, the team reflects on how to become more effective, then tunes and adjusts its behavior accordingly.**

This principle is the reason why a Scrum must engage in the Daily Standup Meeting, Sprint Review Meeting, and the Sprint Retrospect Meeting. These meetings allow the team to assess where they are and where they want to go. In doing so on a regular basis, the team is able to determine what changes need to be made in order for it to work at optimal levels.

How to Embrace Agile Principles in Your Organization

Your organization can embrace Agile principles today. However, actually implementing them is not easy. It is at this point that you, and your organization, may consider hiring a consultant such as an Agile Coach, take a class in the way of Agile and Scrum methodology, or simply read up about the topic.

The shift toward the Agile mindset requires an institutional understanding in which the majority of members are committed toward developing a much better process of doing things. This would imply the organization realizing that there is no need to hold authority over anybody and that collaboration is the key to success. At the end of the day, any organization that truly wishes to become Agile may do so by embracing these principles and actively implementing.

So, take the time to learn as much as you can about them and then finding the right way to implement them based on your organization's own characteristics and idiosyncrasies.

7

Best practices for Scrum Practitioners

I n this chapter, we will take a look at some best practices that Scrum practitioners can put to practice, either as part of a project or as a part of their usual, daily business.

Being a Scrum practitioner implies living the Agile mindset to the fullest. Since the Agile mindset has a structured way of going about things, it's worth making a point of how important being open and flexible is under the Scrum umbrella.

So, the most important thing that any Scrum practitioner can do is become as well-versed as possible in the way of Scrum. Tools designed for learning about Scrum, such as this one, will provide anyone who is interested in learning about Scrum a plethora of information and knowledge.

Now, let's dig a bit deeper and have a look at some of the tips and advice that Scrum practitioners can put into practice in further developing their knowledge regarding Scrum and Agile.

Constant learning

This first tip is, by far, the most important. If you choose to do one thing, this is it.

When you have committed to lifelong learning, you will always find a way to improve things. Sure, lifelong learning doesn't just apply to one aspect of life. It applies to a number of aspects which can be learned and implemented in life.

As such, maintaining constant learning about Scrum and Agile methodologies, practices, and techniques should enable you to pick and choose the aspects which you feel can better improve your skills in addition to those of your team.

Constant learning can happen through self-teaching such as through videos, online courses, and books. It can also apply to have discussions with other Scrum practitioners, or simply "talking shop" with other team members.

At the end of the day, whatever you choose to do to further your skills will go a long way toward helping you become the most effective practitioner you can be. It will certainly pay off for you to invest your time and efforts into deepening your understanding of all things Agile.

Constant teaching

As with constant learning, constant teaching will help you improve your team's overall skillset. As a potential leader within the Scrum domain, you will have the opportunity to share your understanding and experience within the domain of the Scrum world.

Given that Scrum is all about a collaborative nature, your team will be able to play a dual role, teaching and learning, and thereby providing feedback to the team. This will enable you to help your team stay on the same page. It is of the utmost importance to keep your team in stride. That way, you will be able to make the most of your opportunities to make your team come together.

So, don't be afraid to play the role of teacher. Just make sure that everyone gets an equal opportunity to play the same role. Bear in mind that everyone has an equal amount of knowledge and experience to share with the team itself. Thus, it is certainly worth including everyone in the teaching and learning process.

Seeking help

This is one of the hardest things to do in life.

Often, many individuals do not seek help out of fear they will be judged in a negative light. So, individual Scrum practitioners may choose to forego getting the help they need in implementing Scrum methodology effectively.

But beyond getting help with Scrum methodology as such, getting help with technical aspects related to the actual project development may be necessary in order to fulfill the customer's expectations. Moreover, certain projects may require very technical expertise. As such, finding subject matter experts who specialize in a given area may be necessary. This is especially true when the organization is looking to implement a product or solution which it has never attempted before.

Adding a subject matter expert on the Scrum team might work well enough. Although, it might also be possible for the Product Owner to sit down with the outside expert, or consultant, and go over what the solution might. Then, the Product Owner would work with the Scrum Master in order to find the right way to incorporate the technical solution into the project's development.

If the team is able to foresee the need for this technical advice, the participation of such an expert may be incorporated in between sprints, or the expert could be included for the sprint, or sprints, in which that knowledge would be needed. Then, the expert could leave the team once their work is done.

The main thing to keep in mind is that whatever the case, the team should not be afraid to seek it. In doing so, the team would be able to ensure that they have what it takes in order to get the job done in the best possible way.

Find a good Agile Coach

Finding a good Agile Coach is essential especially when an organization is implementing Scrum for the first time. While the Product Owner and the Scrum Master may be experienced in the ways of Scrum, they may not feel entirely confident in leading a change process. So, a good Agile Coach fits in well since this coach will enable a fledgling Scrum team to truly hit their stride.

Now, in the case where a project team is completely new to Scrum, then a good Agile coach becomes even more important. There might be cases in which an organization is sold on the virtues of Scrum, but may not have any staff members who are experienced. So, the Agile Coach can mentor the team from the sidelines until they are ready to take on an entire project on their own.

Furthermore, the Agile coach may choose to take the entire

project team through the project procedure or work with individuals such as the Scrum Master throughout the execution of a sprint, or an entire project.

Also, the Agile Coach may work with the Development Team on a sprint, or even throughout an entire project, in order for them to get the feel for the way a properly run project should be conducted. Ultimately, this implies providing the Development Team with the tools and know-how they would need over the course of a regular sprint.

So, getting on board with a good Agile Coach will certainly help the project team immensely.

Lessons Learned

At the end of a sprint and a project, the Scrum team may decide to record their lessons learned as a part of the Sprint Retrospect Meeting. This record is essentially a description of a challenge and how it was overcome or what was learned from a given situation.

So, the Scrum team can choose to record events in such a way that they provide a memoir of how things can go wrong, mistakes that can be made and how these will affect the overall performance of the team.

Consequently, the Scrum team will have an archive of practical examples of what can happen to them throughout the course of a project. Hence, lessons learned is an ideal way of helping a team grow so that they avoid making the same mistakes over and over. In addition, lessons learned can help a team build a wealth of knowledge and experience that will ultimately allow them to find new ways of approaching a constant situation.

8

Stories from the Trenches

One of the things which we have pointed out throughout the course of this book is how Scrum is not limited to software development. Sure, Scrum emerged from the software development and IT world, but the methodology, as such, is not limited to just this domain.

As a matter of fact, Scrum can be implemented in virtually any type of field or area of knowledge. In particular, it is ideal for those projects which have a high degree of volatility or uncertainty.

What would make a project volatile and uncertain?

Well, one simple example of an uncertain and volatile project would be running a project that's never been done before... at least for your organization.

In such cases, there are a lot of instances regarding change, modifications, and trial and error. So, Scrum becomes a great way of dealing with the uncertainty of producing something that your organization may not have attempted before.

Consider the following example.

ABC Corporation, a large pharmaceutical company, has traditionally specialized in producing medication to treat diabetes. However, this pharmaceutical is looking to build an entirely new treatment for hypertension.

This pharmaceutical has very experienced doctors and researchers. It's just that they never tried to build a drug for hypertension. Now, the reason for embarking on this project is due to the fact that the company's board has decided to expand into a market that they feel is underserved.

So, the board has tasked the CEO with getting the project off the ground. This makes the company's board as the project sponsor as they are the ones who are looking to get this project done, while the CEO becomes the project's customer.

The CEO has now tasked the Head of the Research Department to become the project manager. Since the Head of the Research Department is an experienced Scrum practitioner, the choice for using Scrum project methodology was clear.

The Head of the Research Department is now the Product Owner. As such, the Product Owner is now in need of finding a good Scrum Master.

For this job, the Product Owner has tapped a senior researcher in the Research Department. This senior member has been on Scrum-based projects before. So, this member is clear on how to run a project, as well as, individual sprints.

The next task is to assemble the Development Team. The Development Team is to be comprised of researchers within the department. In total, a team of 6 researchers has been assembled to take on this project. The reason for the size of this team is because the Product Owner wants to assemble researchers with various types of expertise.

Now, the Scrum Master has assembled the team to work on the user stories for this project. The reason for having the entire team work together on crafting the user stories is because of this a project that has never been done before. So, the Product Owner is keen on making sure that everyone is on board with the project.

Once the user stories have been crafted, it's time to create the Product Backlog. In this Backlog, the entire team has worked together on determining which items need to be completed in order for the entire project to come together. As such, the Product Owner has asked the Development

Team to brainstorm all of the tasks that they feel will be needed in order to craft the final product.

Next, the Scrum Master works with the Development Team to whittle down the brainstormed ideas into a single list of the tasks needed for the project. These tasks have been divided into "essential" and "non-essential". So, that means that the essential tasks are absolutely necessary in order to comply with the customer's specifications. In this case, the CEO has given the Head of the Research Departments the guidelines that they need to follow in order to ensure the acceptance criteria for this project.

Once the team has determined which tasks are absolutely necessary for this project, the next step becomes deciding if the non-essential tasks are worth keeping or getting rid of. One example of a non-essential task could be developing a marketing plan for the new medication. The reason for this consideration is because the pharmaceutical may decide to get a marketing company to put this plan together. Or, the company may choose to run a separate Scrum project for the marketing portion.

With a finalized Product Backlog, it is now time to run the first Sprint Planning Meeting. In this initial Sprint Planning Meeting, the Scrum team can choose how to divide up work so that the number of sprints can be determined. For the sake of simplicity, the team has decided that in order to fulfill all of the user stories and complete the Product Backlog, there is a need for 10, 5-week sprints. This means that the project will take a grand total of 50 weeks.

Based on the scope of the project, the Scrum team has decided that they will break up the items on the Product Backlog in such a way that the most important tasks will be done first. These are the task which will lay the foundation so that the new medication can begin testing at some point mid-way through the project.

Once the Product Backlog and the number of sprints have been decided, the Scrum team has now decided which items it will tackle first. These items are compiled and turned into the Sprint Backlog for the first sprint.

In this first spring, the Burndown Chart has been specifically developed so as to match the Sprint Backlog. This provides the Scrum team with the necessary discipline in order to know exactly when certain tasks need to be completed.

Finally, the sprint gets underway. The team works on the items in the Sprint Backlog and delivers the output of the first sprint which is a design for the new medication. So, when the design is complete, the team is now ready to move onto the next sprint in which the medication will actually be built.

At the end of the sprint, the Scrum team will hold the first Sprint Review Meeting. In this meeting, the Scrum team will present their design for the new medication. The CEO and the board will see the new design and make their comments on it and provide feedback. Based on the feedback, there may be change requests which need to be incorporated into the next sprint.

After the Sprint Review Meeting, the Sprint Retrospect Meeting takes place. In this meeting, the Scrum team will sit down to go over all of the events that took place during the sprint. This is the chance for the Scrum to debrief and incorporate the feedback which was provided to the team at the Sprint Review Meeting. The change requests, if any, are incorporated into the planning for the following sprint, or whenever it is appropriate.

The team will then segue into the next Sprint Planning Meeting. In this meeting, the work is broken down and laid out for the subsequent sprint. The team is now all set and ready to go for the following sprint. The process is then repeated into what is now the second iteration.

In this example, the Scrum team has gone from the outset of the project to the completion of the first sprint. As you can see, the process by which the Scrum team has managed to complete its first set of objectives. Eventually, the team will be able to provide a working prototype of the medication for testing. Then, the testing should end up providing a final product release. Considering that this is a medication we're talking about, the final closing of the project would be related to the official authorization for the medication's commercialization.

With the product finalized, high-fives will go around, and the celebration may begin in another project successfully completed.

Conclusion

Well, if you have made it to this point, it is because you are serious about Scrum.

As we have discussed earlier, Scrum is a rather simple methodology to implement but it takes time to master it. Not only does Scrum require a fair amount of work in developing working proficiency, but it is certainly worth it.

I would greatly encourage you to put in the time and effort into mastering your project management skills. As such, Scrum can help you get the right skills and the right people you need in order to make the most out of your endeavors. Best of all, Scrum is the type of methodology you can implement virtually anywhere at any time.

At this point, it is time for you to get your feet wet in the Scrum world. As you gain experience, you will be able to improve your knowledge and understanding with each iteration of the process. In addition, the lessons learned that you are able to collect will help you to build a working doctrine in your particular field.

So, what's the next step?

If your organization is considering the implementation of Scrum as a project management methodology or just a regular business practice, then, by all means, share this information with your colleagues and business associates.

You can begin by discussing how Scrum can benefit your organization. Granted, it should be said that Scrum may not be ideal for everyone. There might be a valid reason why Scrum may be ideal for your organization. Notwithstanding, you can get together with your colleagues and figure out how Scrum can help you improve your overall business processes.

Best of all, you can begin to implement the use of Scrum in an incremental fashion. That means that it does not have to be an overnight process. By incrementally implementing Scrum, you can find your bearings slowly. As you build up your experience and understanding of Scrum and Agile, you will be able to put it to work for you and your organization.

Ultimately, your efforts will lead you to learn more about you and your organization. You will learn how you can improve your organization's overall processes and business practices.

If you have found this book to be interesting and informative, please share it with your colleagues and business associates. Also, don't forget to leave a comment. I am sure that other like-minded individuals will find your comments to be useful. There are others out there who may have heard of Scrum but are not sure what it is. So, your input will certainly be appreciated by many folks who are wondering if Scrum is right for them and their organization.

I hope that this book has met your expectations. It was written with great care and patience. Should you have any questions or any comments, I would be glad to hear about it. If anything, engaging in a useful discussion will help us all learn more about Scrum and how it can be refined and improved over time.

Thanks again for reading.

CPSIA information can be obtained
at www.ICGtesting.com
Printed in the USA
BVHW061012140720
583698BV00008B/373

9 781087 864884